Recruiting for High Performance

Attracting the Best

Robert W. Wendover

A Crisp Fifty-Minute™ Series Book

This Fifty-Minute™ book is designed to be "read with a pencil." It is an excellent workbook for self-study as well as classroom learning. All material is copyright-protected and cannot be duplicated without permission from the publisher. *Therefore, be sure to order a copy for every training participant by contacting:*

THOMSON

NETg

1-800-442-7477 • 25 Thomson Place, Boston MA • www.courseilt.com

Recruiting for High Performance

Attracting the Best

Robert W. Wendover

CREDITS:

Product Manager: **Debbie Woodbury**
Editor: **Brenda Pittsley**
Production Editor: **Genevieve McDermott**
Production Artists: **Nicole Phillips, Rich Lehl, and Betty Hopkins**
Manufacturing: **Stephanie Porreca**
Cartoonist: **Ralph Mapson**

Trademarks
Crisp Fifty-Minute Series is a trademark of NETg. Some of the product names and company names used in this book have been used for identification purposes only, and may be trademarks or registered trademarks of their respective manufacturers and sellers.

Disclaimer
NETg reserves the right to revise this publication and make changes from time to time in its content without notice.

ISBN 1-56052-686-6
Library of Congress Catalog Card Number 2002112499
Printed in the United States

2 3 4 5 GP 08 07 06

Learning Objectives For:

RECRUITING FOR HIGH PERFORMANCE

The objectives for *Recruiting for High Performance* are listed below. They have been developed to guide the user to the core issues covered in this book.

THE OBJECTIVES OF THIS BOOK ARE TO HELP THE USER:

1) Explore a wide range of sources to fill labor needs

2) Identify strategies for attracting qualified applicants

3) Design and implement an effective recruiting effort

ASSESSING PROGRESS

NETg has developed a Crisp Series **assessment** that covers the fundamental information presented in this book. A 25-item, multiple-choice and true/false questionnaire allows the reader to evaluate his or her comprehension of the subject matter. To download the assessment and answer key, go to www.courseilt.com and search on the book title, or call 1-800-442-7477.

Assessments should not be used in any employee selection process.

About the Author

Robert W. Wendover has been writing and speaking on the topic of recruiting employees for the past 16 years. The author of five books, his work has appeared in publications as varied as *The Wall Street Journal's National Business Employment Weekly* and *Convenience Store News*. He appears regularly in electronic media including CNN, CNBC, and an array of local stations around the U.S. His clients include Kinko's, Sears, State Farm Insurance, Kaiser Permanente, and a host of other household names. He has also served on the management faculty of the University of Phoenix for the past 10 years.

How to Use This Book

This *Fifty-Minute™ Series Book* is a unique, user-friendly product. As you read through the material, you will quickly experience the interactive nature of the book. There are numerous exercises, real-world case studies, and examples that invite your opinion, as well as checklists, tips, and concise summaries that reinforce your understanding of the concepts presented.

A Crisp Learning *Fifty-Minute™ Book* can be used in a variety of ways. Individual self-study is one of the most common. However, many organizations use *Fifty-Minute* books for pre-study before a classroom training session. Other organizations use the books as a part of a systemwide learning program—supported by video and other media based on the content in the books. Still others work with Crisp Learning to customize the material to meet their specific needs and reflect their culture. Regardless of how it is used, we hope you will join the more than 20 million satisfied learners worldwide who have completed a *Fifty-Minute Book*.

Preface

Recruiting isn't what it used to be. We can no longer hang a sign or run an advertisement and expect the best people to beat a path to our door. Many of today's applicants have concluded, right or wrong, that they are in the driver's seat when it comes to hiring. Because of the historically low unemployment rate, individuals have learned that they can "shop" for a job, at least in certain industries. Unfortunately, some employers have succumbed to the temptation of raising wages simply to fill the slots with people who are "upright, warm, and breathing." As one can imagine, this has done little more than reinforce any unreasonable perceptions of applicants.

The new generations of applicants are also more skeptical of the employer/employee relationship than ever before. They have watched their friends and family members get laid off, companies consolidate, and the economy shift more than once. For these reasons, they view jobs more as a contract as opposed to a calling. When they discover that your organization is hiring, their first question might very well be "What's in it for me?"

It takes more than a simple posting these days to attract the kind of people you want to fill the positions within your organization. This book is targeted to those responsible for attracting applicants who will be good matches for the jobs you have. Recruiting has become more complicated than ever before and *Recruiting for High Performance* has been written to teach you, the reader, how to design and implement an ongoing campaign that is both successful and cost-effective.

This book is not filled with theory, but a down-to-earth approach that you, the manager or supervisor, can use immediately. So, let's get on with it!

Robert W. Wendover

Robert W. Wendover

Contents

Part 1: Reaching Out for Applicants

Part 2: Labor Sources

Part 3: Organizing an External Recruiting Plan

Part 4: Implementing Your Recruiting Plan

Summary

Recruiting the Best

Recruiting for High Performance is about attracting the best people to your organization. In today's labor market, recruiters are challenged to look to diverse population groups and to use creative recruitment techniques to find quality employees.

Hiring is most effective when recruiters have a sufficient pool of high-caliber candidates from which to choose the best people for specific jobs. This requires focus and organization on the part of the recruiter, plus a willingness to experiment with methods, research, and incentive programs. In doing this, it is important to remember that while you are evaluating prospective employees, they are also evaluating your company. A company that maintains a high profile and seems desirable to work for will attract more qualified candidates. Employee selection is not a one-sided event.

If you want to find out more about effective hiring for your job openings, read *High Performance Hiring,* the companion title to this book, available from Crisp Publications.

The Recruiting Skills Inventory

To examine the hiring and retention procedures in your organization, it is helpful to conduct a recruiting skills inventory. The following questions address the major considerations of a successful recruiting effort.

1 Have you defined the type of person who excels in your organization?

Examine the culture. What motivates your top performers? How well do people get along? Is this a serious atmosphere or is it more fun loving? How important are people skills in your business? Make a list of the characteristics you think are necessary for success in your organization. Share it with others and ask them to add their thoughts. The resulting factors can comprise a checklist of what to look for in your new hires.

2 Have you surveyed your present employees to find out why they applied?

Front-line people can usually provide more insight into potential applicants' motivations than those farther up the ladder. Ask them about the people they know. Ask them what advice they would give someone who showed interest in the organization. Then incorporate that knowledge in the organization's recruiting efforts.

3 Do you know where your applicants come from?

Few organizations take the time to find out how applicants learn of their company. A $2000 newspaper ad is a poor investment if it results in only a handful of applications. On the other hand, a discreetly placed promotion placed with local community leaders may result in a considerable number of qualified applicants with no cash expense involved. Unless you take the time to ask applicants where they heard about the opening and then track that information, you run the risk of wasting time and money.

4 Are you reaching the right applicant sources with the right messages?

People apply for positions because of what's in it for them, not what's in it for the organization. Are your advertisements and promotions attracting people the way they want to be attracted? If not, the efforts will fall on deaf ears.

5 Do you track recruiting costs?

How much did it cost to replace the last receptionist who left the organization? With employee turnover running into thousands of dollars, no organization can afford to be sloppy with its hiring. Calculating turnover and recruiting costs brings home the seriousness of conducting employee selection with care.

Have you "deputized" everyone as a recruiter?

Each person who works for the organization may be approached by a potential applicant. Why not prepare everyone by providing the information they need to make a good impression? Recruiting brochures and company literature will help them answer basic questions and refer applicants to the right people within your organization.

Do you continually cultivate new sources of applicants?

Many companies have watched the bottoms fall out of their applicant pools thanks to a diminishing number of high-school-age workers. Technical managers are also scrambling because of the scarcity of skilled personnel. Developing new and consistent labor sources requires new ways of recruiting and new types of employees. Do not wait for one source to dry up before pursuing another. The public relations and marketing you do in your community should include recruiting. Applications should be tracked and candidates should be queried about how they learned of positions. Following is a sample recruiting report to help you track these sources.

RECRUITING REPORT

Position title: _____   Number of openings: _____

Sources:

Type	Cost of using source	Yield	Comments
In-house posting			
Classified ads			
Employee referrals			
Agency (private)			
Agency (public)			
Other			

General recommendations: _____

_____

---

8 Are you considering the versatility of candidates?

While most people are hired to perform one role, many end up doing a variety of tasks. Are you looking for individuals who readily adapt to new responsibilities and challenges?

9 Are you studying your competitors' recruiting techniques?

Do you know what your competitors are doing to locate applicants? How are they retaining the best performers? Look for their advertisements. Talk to any of your employees who have worked for them. Listen closely at professional and industry meetings. Figure out which of their ideas would work for you.

10 Are you the company to work for?

Has your company developed a reputation as an organization that treats its employees well? Is the word on the street that people working for you succeed? This type of public relations goes a long way toward both attracting applicants and retaining employees. You want your employees to be proud of where they work. Learn to sell your best candidates on how working for you can be a good move for them.

While this list is not all-inclusive, it should give you a working knowledge of the key components of recruiting for high performance. Notice that the points are not all mechanical. They involve focus, philosophy, and a general understanding of human nature. Selection processes that are too mechanical neglect the understanding needed to select not just a qualified person, but the right person for the job.

Reaching Out for

Applicants

2

Developing a Recruiting Policy

Do you have the applicants you need when you need them? Labor sources throughout the United States are changing. The overall population is aging. Growth in the labor force will come primarily from minority groups.

Your ability to anticipate and react to changes in the work force ensures successful recruiting. But how can this be accomplished?

You can begin by developing a clearly defined recruiting philosophy. Determine what qualities are needed for every position so you can draw a picture of the right recruit. In addition, the company should have recruiting goals and a means for communicating these goals to all employees.

Remember that candidates are screening you as much as you are screening them. Employees are much more concerned about their ability to control their environment within the workplace than they have been in the past. If your employees feel unable to control their surroundings, the growing scarcity of workers will allow them to simply vote with their feet and move to another employer.

A key ingredient for effective recruiting is being able to offer better work environments coupled with flexible benefits and generous training opportunities. Companies that are able to implement these changes become flexible work sites and become the most successful employers.

Accommodating Diversity

As the labor force changed over the years, employers faced new challenges and opportunities. Forward-looking employers took advantage of the changes by targeting diverse population groups to staff their businesses. Employers who included people of color, recent immigrants, senior workers, and individuals with disabilities in their candidate search were more successful at hiring and retaining quality employees.

As an employer your ability to adapt to these groups and to take advantage of their interests, experience, and work ethic will serve to strengthen your standing within the industry and community.

A shift in generations has also changed the workforce. While older generations "lived to work," young people are more interested in "working to live." Employers are discovering that younger applicants are assertive about asking questions regarding working conditions, corporate strength, opportunities for advancement, and training. Interviewers need to be prepared for more give-and-take rather than simply question-and-answer.

Another challenge facing some employers is the growing number of applicants who speak English as a second language. While some argue that English should be the only language spoken at a work site, reality indicates that you, the employer, must be able to communicate clearly with all employees, if for no other reason than safety. An employer's willingness to work toward a common solution not only increases communication, but demonstrates flexibility and an orientation toward teamwork.

In addition to language, other issues to consider when recruiting a diverse workforce include cultural heritage, levels and types of education, experience, and balance of life issues. When interviewing candidates, all of these factors enter in, whether or not the employer is aware of it. Applicants hire you as much as you hire them; therefore, your ability to communicate concern and sincerity about their welfare is of paramount importance.

If you are dealing with applicants from diverse backgrounds, consider what you can do to accommodate them during the interview process. Place yourself in their shoes and consider their concerns and apprehensions about your hiring process. Keep a list of factors such as language barriers, cultural concerns, reading levels, understanding of language nuances and social norms, appearance, dress, and the like. Then strive to address each of these issues.

For additional perspective on diversity in the workplace, read *Working Together* by George Simons, Crisp Publications.

Picturing the Right Recruit

With the wide variety of people who apply to your company, it is difficult to determine who will be the best fit for open positions. Developing a clear profile of the people who succeed in your company will help you to select from those who complete applications.

While the desired skills may vary, successful candidates must share the same general values of current employees. Look around your organization and take stock of the present work force. What kind of work style do they have? Is it fast paced? Are they more deliberate? Are they jovial or are they a solemn group?

What about the workplace itself? Is it noisy? Can people concentrate? What are management expectations concerning performance and individual contribution? These, and a host of other factors all need to be considered. This composite picture will provide you with a guide for identifying compatible applicants.

Setting recruiting goals enables you to develop the sources you need for the future. If a particular area experiences higher turnover or greater expansion, promoting these openings on an informal basis, in advance, eases the task when the actual need arises.

Review past hiring patterns. Are there certain times of the year when your company experiences higher turnover? Do employees with certain backgrounds or experiences seem to be the ones that always leave? These might be the type of individuals to avoid recruiting. Have employees with particular skills or experience succeeded better than the average? These are individuals you want to pursue. Noting these patterns will enhance your recruiting efforts.

Once these goals have been established, they must be communicated to everyone in the organization. Since reliable employees often come from internal referrals, it is imperative that all employees know about openings you are seeking to fill.

Determining Needs

Consider the following ideas when developing your list of needs:

➤ **Consult the job description for the position.** In addition to identifying actual duties, look for other attributes that might be helpful.

➤ **Determine the characteristics of your organization's culture.** What attributes might a person need to fit in?

➤ **Who will be supervising the position?** What attributes should a person possess to serve as a complement to this boss?

➤ **With what other individuals will this person have day-to-day contact?** Are there certain group characteristics that need to be taken into account?

➤ **Look around your environment.** What other factors might have to be taken into consideration to ensure a thorough assessment of position characteristics?

This type of procedure should be followed with each hire. While it can be time consuming, it tends to ensure effective hiring, low turnover, and higher productivity.

For more information on defining job requirements, read *Behavior-Based Interviewing* by Terry Fitzwater, Crisp Publications.

The Recruiting Plan

While there is no exact way to determine optimum strategies for recruiting in every position, you should develop a plan prior to approaching applicant pools. Comparing the actual results with the original estimates will provide an approximate picture of your effectiveness.

Here are some considerations:

➤ What positions are you presently seeking to fill?

➤ Which of these jobs can benefit from the same advertising?

➤ Which of these jobs should not be advertised with others? (i.e., do not cluster shop foremen with accountants.)

➤ What is the expected turnover? If you are expecting high turnover, as in retail, your standards for acceptable applicants may be lower than for a long-term professional.

➤ Who are your targeted applicant pools? Applicants for different positions will be recruited from different sources.

➤ What are the best strategies for approaching the pools selected?

➤ What staff resources will be necessary to complete this project?

➤ How far in advance will you have to recruit to fill upcoming vacancies? Develop a time line.

➤ What are the recruiting messages being used with different applicant pools? Try not to mix these strategies. It will confuse people.

➤ Does your plan include the recruiting of minorities and other protected classes?

➤ Are the strategies proposed consistent with your organization's image? Would you advertise for bank tellers on bumper stickers, for instance? Consider how your recruiting tactics will reflect on your company's reputation.

➤ What will the recruiting campaign cost? Be sure to include expenses such as staff time, postage, and phone charges.

➤ What approvals are necessary for this project to begin? Be sure to build support among those who hold the necessary influence.

Develop a flow chart to organize the actual process. Keeping an eye on the process graphically will help you stay on top of the plan's implementation.

Plan Evaluation

The effectiveness of recruiting plans can be measured in several different ways:

➤ **Cost per hire is determined by dividing the total expense of the plan by the number of hires.**

➤ **Be sure to include all indirect expenses such as clerical and planning time.** Calculating cost per hire enables you to analyze your effectiveness in hiring quality candidates economically.

➤ **Vacancy rates allow recruiters to evaluate the patterns of frequency in employee turnover.** It is calculated by dividing the number of open positions by the total number of positions when the organization is fully staffed. This information can be instrumental in discovering escalating turnover among certain jobs.

➤ **Selection rates enable you to see the ratio between the number of people interviewed and the number hired.** This information is obtained by dividing the number of interviews by the number of hires. Selection rates help you to determine the quality of the candidates being interviewed. If your selection rate is low, your pre-interview screening techniques may need to be evaluated.

➤ **Response rates illustrate the return on recruiting advertisements.** A low return means that the effectiveness of the ad needs to be improved. Response rates are calculated by dividing the number of people who responded to the ad by the number who were actually qualified for the position. If, for example, you receive 200 responses to a particular campaign and only 25 are qualified, the targeting of the ad probably needs adjustment.

Recruiting plans, if carefully developed, can be extremely valuable in conducting a quality and cost-efficient recruiting campaign. In addition, plans such as this ensure compliance with equal opportunity and affirmative action requirements. Following is a sample recruiting plan memo that shows you a breakdown of several different recruiting options.

To: Jackie Toon, Operations Manager
From: Alex Quick, Recruiting Coordinator
Re: Recruiting plan for shipping, distributing, and telemarketing

After consulting with all departments involved and doing some research on the local labor market, I've developed a plan to increase our number of applicants. Below are the strategies I plan to use along with the dollar cost and projections for how many applicants will result over a period of one month.

Local Job Training Programs

	Dollar Cost	Projected applicants
Direct mail to selected customers	$ 300	15
Newspaper display ads	1500	75
Employee referral campaign	550	65
Local Job Training Partnership Act program	25	15
Signs on local transit	400	40
Morning radio spots	600	50
Posters at all 7 community colleges	100	70
Letters to churches and senior centers	50	100
Estimated totals	$3525	430

Estimated cost per applicant = $8.20

Locating Internal Candidates

Internal candidates and applicants referred by employees are the most cost-efficient way of filling vacancies. With the promotion of a current employee you get a person who already knows the organization while proving to other employees that there are opportunities for moving up. Applicants referred by employees will probably be more reliable since the reputation of the referring employee is at stake. When making promotions and encouraging referrals, you should clearly explain how people will be considered. Referrals are not an automatic hire.

If an employee is under consideration for promotion into an open position, that person must understand there is no guarantee the promotion will be given to the internal candidate. Misunderstandings can result in hard feelings and damaged employee morale.

The best way to handle referrals and promotions is to develop a plan of action:

➢ **Communicate clearly to all employees.** This minimizes rumors and misunderstandings.

➢ **Design a workable referral and promotion system.** Consider how long vacancies should be posted in order to give employees a chance to respond. Make sure everyone involved knows how the system works. Set standards that are fair to all. Avoid any appearance of favoritism.

➢ **If you are considering someone from another department for a position, notify the employee's current supervisor of the possible move.** Protocol requires that the current boss be informed. "Stealing" employees creates animosity. Besides, the supervisor might be able to shed some additional light on the person's performance and potential.

➢ **Record the names of people who make referrals and the people they referred.** If some have a better track record than others, go back to them with vacancies. If certain people suggest people who are poor matches, you probably should avoid their referrals in the future.

➢ **Reward those who make good referrals.** This encourages them to continue and encourages others as well.

➢ **Set internal promotion goals.** Decide how many positions you would like to fill internally each year, and then encourage internal applications. If employees see there is a chance to move up, it may inspire increased productivity.

Identifying Applicants' Motivations

As you develop a strategy for recruiting applicants, it helps to investigate the motivations of the groups you are pursuing. By tailoring your recruiting message you will receive a better response in less time with fewer dollars. This can be accomplished in several ways.

The most basic strategy is to simply list those attitudes likely to appear in your target audience. If you have the same experience, age, and background, you should be able to develop an accurate profile of recruiting materials and approaches.

In many cases, however, those doing the recruiting and those being recruited vary significantly in age, values, and experience. While it's true you were once 18, that does not mean you can identify with the attitudes of today's teenager. A means for getting more accurate information is to ask the teenagers already working for you. This not only provides useful input, but also involves them in the process. Their ensuing interest may result in more enthusiasm for the job and even referrals of qualified applicants.

A final method is actually surveying those in your target groups. This means getting on the phone and asking them what they want out of a job opportunity. While this can be time-consuming and expensive, it may result in good referrals and useful information. Going directly to the market will also help enhance your organization's image.

Here are some sample questions:

"What is the most important feature to you in a job?"

"What was your last job?" or "Where are you working now?"

"Why did you accept that job?"

"What did you like most about your last job?"

"What did you like least about your last job?"

"What is the most important feature you look for in a supervisor?"

"How did you find out about your last job?"

"Please rank the following from most to least important: distance to work, hours, job duties, pay, work environment."

Once you develop a feeling for applicants' motivations, you are ready to launch a recruiting effort. Compare the information in the job description with the applicants' motivations to determine the target groups. Now you are ready to decide on the best strategies for reaching these applicants.

The summary section of this book lists strategies that organizations have used to attract applicants. Combine this list with the methods mentioned above and budget for the most effective campaign.

Research and planning are key to any recruiting strategy. Even if an opening is a sudden vacancy, plans should be in place to access the appropriate groups of likely candidates. An ongoing effort to locate the best applicants is the secret to recruiting success.

Enhancing the Company Image

Before commencing a recruiting program, it's a good idea to examine how your company is perceived in the community. Recruiting efforts yield few results if there are questions about an organization's integrity, how it treats its employees, or a host of other situations.

The best way to determine your company's image is to ask around. Conduct an informal survey by asking those in the community questions such as:

"What have you heard about our organization?"

"Do you know what products we make? Do you use them?"

"Do you know anyone who works for our organization?"

"What are your impressions, based on what they have said?"

In addition to finding out the public's perception, you may learn some new things about the organization you did not know. Someone may even suggest better ideas for reaching the applicants you want.

Here are some points to keep in mind when trying to enhance the organization's image:

➤ **Overall company public relations.** Be sure that those serving in the company's public relations function are informed about recruiting efforts. Provide them with as much information as possible on hiring and training endeavors and how these relate to community outreach.

➤ **Recruiting literature.** Top-notch materials explaining the company and its opportunities are a powerful way to impress applicants. Confusing or poorly produced materials will have negative results on your efforts. Consider matching the media to your target audience and producing an effective brochure, poster, video, CD, or Web site.

➤ **Reception of collateral.** How are applicants treated when they make contact with your company? Is the receptionist well informed about openings and procedures? Are candidates treated professionally? That first impression goes a long way toward selling the job and the company.

➤ **Handling the selection process.** Do candidates understand the process? Is it timely and kept on course? Are interviewers prepared? Do you make an effort to "sell" the top candidate? It's the little things that make or break a recruiting effort.

➤ **Employee turnover.** What do former employees say about your organization? Those who talk about long hours, difficult supervisors, or confusing priorities damage the company's image. This is a perfect reason to work toward better retention.

16

P A R T 2

Labor Sources

18

Exploring Sources of Labor

The major change in recruiting has been the evolution of labor sources. For years, employers took the ample supply of labor for granted. Much of this supply has consisted of students and homemakers looking for part-time work.

But as the baby boom generation has grown up and the number of career women has exploded, employers have found themselves short-handed. Every industry is experiencing the crunch for qualified applicants.

When labor sources are in short supply, we need to pay more attention to groups that have received a prejudicial eye in the past. These include:

➤ Senior workers (those 55 and over)

➤ Displaced homemakers

➤ Moonlighters

➤ Retired or exiting military

➤ Career changers

➤ Individuals with physical disabilities

➤ Individuals with mental disabilities

➤ Ex-offenders

➤ Economically disadvantaged

Senior Workers

The largest and most influential alternate source of labor is senior workers. Where 20 years ago most individuals retired at 65, many are now continuing in their jobs or taking early retirement to pursue a new endeavor.

According to a survey conducted by the American Association of Retired Persons, 48% of those who said they were retired indicated that they would consider employment if the right situation appeared. This percentage is predicted to rise dramatically as the Baby Boom generation reaches this milestone. As our population matures, the influence this group will exert in the workforce will be enormous.

While myths surround the capabilities of older workers, most employers are finding these individuals work just as hard and efficiently as their younger counterparts. Due to maturity and experience, they are able to adapt quickly to new responsibilities, deal with crises, and get along with co-workers. Their loyalty to the company also tends to exceed that of younger employees.

The myth that you have to pay an older worker more money has also been found to be untrue. While there are some who command a superior wage, many choose other forms of compensation such as more time off, flexible hours, and health benefits.

Concerns about older workers tend to revolve around their ability to adapt to technology and perceptions of inflexibility and lack of aggressiveness. While some employers are also troubled about potential lost time due to illness, statistics show that older workers and younger workers lose about the same number of days. Retirees and older workers in general may be just what your company needs to maintain a reliable and relatively inexpensive staff.

Accessing the Senior Market

To recruit older workers, the message must be tailored to their way of thinking. Appealing to job qualities they value will attract attention. These include flexible hours, flexible benefits, autonomy, and opportunity to meet new friends and work with people their own age. You might also stress that you value their maturity and experience.

The vehicles for reaching this group are varied:

➤ Advertising in banks and post offices, especially around the first of the month

➤ Community or church publications

➤ Bargain newspapers found at grocery stores

➤ Bulletin boards in communities where there is a concentration of older individuals

➤ Testimonials of older workers within your organization

➤ Posters with tear-off coupons in malls

➤ Advertising in newspaper sections that appeal to older individuals

➤ Local senior centers

There are also an increasing number of retiree pools to be found in cities around the United States. You cannot advertise for "older workers" since this is discriminatory. Many cities have Forty-Plus clubs to assist members in pursuing employment. In general, these are networking organizations for older workers who have been laid off by other companies.

The Small Business Administration's Senior Corps of Retired Executives (SCORE) might also be able to assist. These individuals are generally retired from business, having started their own companies in the past. Not only do they meet with likely candidates every day, but they themselves might be interested in working on at least a contract basis.

Examine the possible sources in your local area and discover how senior workers might fit into your organization.

Displaced Homemakers

Displaced homemakers are those women (and sometimes men) who choose to reenter the workforce after a long period of separation or those who are forced to work due to hardship. In some cases, these individuals have substantial skills and expertise. In others, they are inexperienced and may be entering the workforce for the first time.

Depending on organizational need, the individuals in this group may be able to fill valuable roles. In most cases, training will be necessary to teach new skills for both job duties and for coping with the balance between business and family.

Women Work: The National Network for Women's Employment (202-467-5366 or www.womenwork.org) provides nationwide assistance to these individuals for training and placement. In addition, local agencies such as the YWCA will be able to identify other organizations that provide assistance.

Moonlighters

While many employers have discouraged moonlighters in the past, this group offers a pool of part-time labor to fill a variety of jobs. The key to attracting these individuals is stressing flexibility in schedules. They can best be reached through advertising aimed at groups such as teachers, police officers, firefighters, skilled trade workers, retail clerks, and other hourly employees. If you are especially interested in part-time workers, you might also try college students, homemakers, and individuals who can spare only part of their day.

An alternative to flexible schedules is job sharing. This allows two individuals to complete the job by arranging their schedules and, at the same time, assuring the employer of a full-time worker.

Some companies have also begun to offer additional part-time positions to their full-time employees. This allows these individuals to earn extra cash and saves the employer the trouble of hiring other individuals. In addition, full-time employees are already invested in the organization and do not require training and orientation on company policy.

Retired or Exiting Military

While employers look upon those leaving the military as an excellent source of skills and experience, many of these individuals find landing a civilian job difficult. Much of this is due to the adjustment into a civilian environment along with the challenge of translating skills into business terminology.

To attract these individuals, you have to approach them in ways with which they can identify. One approach is to share testimonials from former military personnel who have joined your firm. You might also consider holding an open house for retiring military, if you are located in an area with a high military concentration.

Advertisements should be written with slogans and terminology that will catch their eye. Phrases such as "Join our team" or "We need your discipline" will attract that split second of attention you need to convince them to read on.

Put military applicants at ease and make them feel welcome when they contact you. Helping them to adjust to an unfamiliar environment will win them over. You might offer a free workshop to help them with their job search in the civilian world. Include some information on opportunities within your organization and how they might fit in.

To reach exiting military personnel, you must advertise in areas they frequent and publications they read. You might, for instance, distribute fliers in stores and housing complexes where there are concentrations of military personnel. A billboard outside a local base will also attract attention.

There are also a number of military publications distributed nationwide. These provide an excellent means for contacting these highly qualified individuals. Call an installation near you for more information.

Career Changers

Those contemplating a career change can be another good source of labor. The average person switches career fields three to four times, and these individuals may be tapped to fill roles in your organization.

While there are plenty of these people outside your organization, there may also be a number inside who are growing restless. Look for better ways to keep those already on board more satisfied with the firm. Cross-training, professional development, and educational assistance all help prevent the loss of key individuals.

One of the best means for attracting career changers is to advertise "little or no training necessary." Many of those contemplating a move may look upon this as an opportunity to gain a foothold in their new area of interest.

Target your recruiting messages to those populations you feel will yield the largest number of respondents. These might include teachers, clerical workers, retail clerks, and manual laborers. There are a number of individuals within these ranks with good skills who are looking for an opportunity to prove themselves.

Avenues for reaching these groups include direct mail, advertisement in publications they read frequently, local clergy, and related business groups.

Individuals with Disabilities

The most underused pool of labor in the United States is working-age adults with disabilities. Even with establishment of the Americans with Disabilities Act, many still find it difficult to secure employment. Even if you want to employ them, in many cases, individuals with disabilities are difficult to locate. Here are some resources:

State Agencies

There are 84 state rehabilitation agencies throughout the nation. These organizations provide training to people with disabilities and help with placement into jobs. In some cases, job coaches are available to assist in the first few weeks of employment.

Most services of these agencies are offered free of charge along with training and equipment to make reasonable accommodation. (Contact the Job Accommodation Network, call 1-800-526-7234 or www.janweb.icdi.wvu.edu.) Public-private partnerships: The Job Training Partnership Act (JTPA) provides training and placement assistance to workers with disabilities through local private industry councils. These councils assess business needs in the community and identify training programs that can provide the necessary individuals. An arrangement is drawn up so that the firms needing workers hire those who meet their qualifications after they are trained according to the organizations' parameters.

Projects with Industry (PWI) is sponsored by the U.S. Department of Education. Industry representatives identify those areas where the greatest job growth is anticipated, and individuals with disabilities are trained to fill those positions. (Contact the U.S. Department of Education, 600 Independence Ave. S.W., Washington, DC 20202 or 202-205-8292.)

Targeted Jobs Tax Credit (TJTC) is a tax incentive for employers who hire workers with disabilities. The program gives employers a credit against first-year's wages paid to the newly hired worker.

Veterans and Private Placement Programs

The Veterans Administration along with some private employment agencies assist with the placement of individuals with disabilities. The local Veterans Administration offices assist employers in locating physically or mentally rehabilitated veterans. In addition, other organizations throughout the United States offer ways to employ individuals with disabilities. Check with local welfare agencies, colleges, and rehabilitation facilities to locate these groups.

Ex-offenders

While the average employer may be hesitant to hire ex-offenders, they are suited for a variety of situations. Although they have been convicted of a felony, they have also paid their debt to society. But this branding tends to make their job search difficult.

In hiring an ex-offender, you will probably obtain a grateful and, therefore, hard-working and loyal employee. In addition, the Targeted Jobs Tax Credit Act provides private employers with wage incentives during the employee's first year. Understandably, an individual of this background should be carefully screened prior to making an offer.

Locating pools of ex-offenders can best be accomplished through state and local rehabilitation programs, job service offices, and agencies within local justice departments. In many cases, these organizations provide job training in addition to placement services.

Economically Disadvantaged

A large, and mostly untapped, source of labor is what the government has defined as the "working poor." These individuals, on welfare programs such as Aid to Families with Dependent Children, choose not to work since they lose health care benefits when employed. However, if your organization provides such benefits to its employees, these individuals may be an excellent source of labor.

While you may have some legitimate concerns about training, attendance, and work ethic, most social services agencies test and train these individuals before they are placed in the job market. In some cases, receipt of benefits is contingent upon the completion of certain programs. While an investment in job training and coping skills may be necessary up front, you will usually be rewarded by loyal employees.

Changes in the Labor Force

The future labor force will be significantly different from today. In addition to a new focus on the groups discussed above, more global considerations are on the horizon. Traditionally, white males have been regarded as the prime group within the labor force because they tend to be more highly educated than minority men and more closely attached to the labor force than women. So-called minority populations have begun to outnumber the majority in certain parts of the country. This is resulting in value changes along with the necessity of being bilingual.

As technology continues to absorb the menial jobs, workers will find knowledge-based positions the only ones available. Since it is becoming apparent that many younger workers lack basic skills and older workers lack computer skills, employers will be forced to assume a much greater role in employee training.

These changes are happening now and will continue into the next century. The organizations that adapt their recruiting to address these changes will be the ones that thrive.

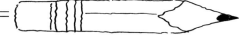

TARGETING NEW LABOR SOURCES

Use this checklist to develop a strategy to expand your candidate search beyond traditional methods and resources. Check (✔) any options that may work for the job opening(s) you have. Add any additional ideas that you might have.

Labor Sources and Where to Find Them

Senior Workers

- ❑ Bulletin boards in: _____
- ❑ Community or church newsletters
- ❑ Advertising circulars at grocery stores
- ❑ Senior center
- ❑ Recreation centers such as golf courses, bowling alleys, and others
- ❑ Other: _____

Displaced Homemakers

- ❑ Bulletin boards in: _____
- ❑ YWCA
- ❑ Women Work or other networking venues
- ❑ Other: _____

Moonlighters

- ❑ Bulletin boards in: _____
- ❑ Community colleges
- ❑ Police precincts and firehouses
- ❑ Grocery stores
- ❑ Other: _____

===CONTINUED===

Retired or Exiting Military

- ❑ Bulletin boards in: _____
- ❑ Ads in military publications
- ❑ Military stores and housing complexes
- ❑ Other: _____

Career Changers

- ❑ Bulletin boards in: _____
- ❑ Retail outlets
- ❑ Community colleges
- ❑ Ads in publications
- ❑ Other: _____

Individuals with Disabilities

- ❑ State agencies
- ❑ Veterans and private placement programs
- ❑ Rehabilitation centers
- ❑ Other: _____

Ex-offenders

- ❑ State and local rehabilitation centers
- ❑ Job placement offices and training organizations
- ❑ Local justice departments
- ❑ Other: _____

Economically Disadvantaged

- ❑ Bulletin boards in: _____
- ❑ Welfare programs
- ❑ Social service agencies
- ❑ Other: _____

32

P A R T 3

Organizing an External Recruiting Plan

34

External Recruiting Sources

There are a number of factors to consider when you choose to recruit externally. Applicants can be recruited through a variety of sources. The position being filled helps dictate which sources you should use.

Sources can be divided into seven categories:

➤ Referral programs

➤ The Internet

➤ Recruiting agencies

➤ Recruiting services

➤ College placement centers

➤ Public job services

➤ Newspaper advertising

A description of each of these sources, and their respective attributes, follows. Before deciding which sources to use, review the job description for the position you seek to fill. Ask yourself what sources are likely to yield appropriate candidates. If you are hiring counter help for instance, newspaper advertisements, college placement centers, and public job services are probably your best bet. On the other hand, locating managers with technical experience can be best accomplished by networking through recruiting services and professional organizations and by announcing the opening in trade journals. The more clearly defined your candidate profile, the better you can target possible applicants.

Use the following descriptions and recommendations for each type of recruiting source to determine what would work best for your organization.

Referral Programs

Whether in times of a labor surplus or a labor shortage, internal referral programs have always been the most effective way to find the best people.

It is a good idea to generate enthusiasm for the referral program by providing incentives and making the results public. Cash awards and other inducements are recommended. Begin by examining employee and associate priorities. All the awards offered should be of approximately the same value and that value should reflect the value you place on hiring good people. A cash reward of $200 is not out of line for a retail referral when the cost of replacing one front-liner has been estimated at $2800. Fast-food gift certificates or tickets to the local boat show won't do. If you want quality referrals, you must provide quality incentives.

Regardless of what you give away as a reward, use the occasion for a celebration. Gather employees at the beginning of a shift, for instance, to introduce new people and publicly welcome them to the team. Then recognize the people who made referrals and present them with their awards. (Make the award contingent on participating in the ceremony.) If the award is a dinner certificate, hand the recipient a restaurant menu with the certificates inside. If it is tickets to a sporting event, hand them a team poster with the tickets attached. If it's a set of new tires, HAND THEM THE TIRES!

The more outrageous the award, the more memorable the event. And the more memorable the event, the more referrals your program will receive.

The Internet

The Internet opened vast new opportunities for organizations to attract applicants for many types of positions. Here are the positive features of Internet recruiting:

- ➤ **It can be free.** Other than the time it takes to develop the promotion, there may be no other costs to post it on your organization's Web site or Web sites owned by cooperating firms. There is a cost to place an ad with online employment sites.

- ➤ **Recruiting is limitless.** Anyone with access to the Internet can see your promotion and respond.

- ➤ **The promotion can be tailored and modified constantly.** If no one responds to the ad, change the headline. If the wrong people respond, make the qualifications more specific. This can be accomplished quickly and with little cost.

- ➤ **The Internet is available 24 hours a day, seven days a week.** This can be a benefit if you are recruiting for positions where potential applicants may be unable to meet with you during normal business hours. Certain shift work jobs are an example.

- ➤ **You can provide more information about the organization and its opportunities than possible in a paper brochure or classified ad.** Without enough information up front, some of the best applicants may not apply.

- ➤ **You can pre-qualify applicants.** By driving applicants to your Web site, you can ask them advance questions that will allow you to prescreen their education, experience, and interest. Applicants who do not meet the qualifications can be sent a polite response thanking them for applying. This saves the time and money of conducting telephone or in-person interviews.

Internet recruiting also has drawbacks:

> **Internet access is not available to all.** While there are thousands of public terminals in libraries and other public places, there are still millions of people who never use them. If you are hiring hourly laborers, for instance, the Internet probably will not yield a sufficient number of interested applicants.

> **It is necessary to drive applicants to your site.** It is easy to post positions on the organization's Web site. Getting people to visit is another thing.

> **You may receive an extraordinary number of inappropriate applications and résumés.** While it is possible to search for thousands of jobs on the World Wide Web, it is also possible to respond to every one of them with the click of a mouse. If your organization is well known, or the positions you offer are a "hot commodity," you may end up with thousands of useless applications.

> **Job search engines may not yield the results you seek.** There is a huge assortment of job-search and posting enterprises ranging from completely generic to industry specific or even job specific. As with any recruiting method, it takes time to research and determine the sites that will best serve your promotions. Even then, constant fine-tuning is required to ensure a stream of quality applicants.

> **You release information to your competitors.** Assume that everything you post online will be examined by those who would delight in poaching your applicants.

How to Begin Recruiting on the Internet

1 **Review online advertisements for positions similar to the ones you seek to fill.**

Accomplish this by visiting Web sites owned by competitors, job-listing services, and industry associations.

2 **Develop a job promotion that addresses the values and requirements of those you want to attract.**

Web users have a short attention span. Remember, they're looking for a job based on their values, not yours or what you think theirs should be. If you don't attract their attention in the first pass, they're lost forever.

3 **Develop a plan for posting the positions.**

Test. Test. Test. Try different sites based on your research. Post jobs on your organization's Web site. Keep the information current with constant monitoring and adjustments.

4 **Develop a plan for driving applicants to your Web site or listing.**

Type any job title into a Web search engine and you will be rewarded with thousands of entries. Leaving your opening at the mercy of search engines is not enough. Your organization's Web site should be included in all of your company's print and electronic promotions. Every person on staff should be able to direct interested parties to the site.

5 **Track your results!**

All applicants should be asked how they heard about the jobs and your organization. This information is crucial to assessing the effectiveness of your recruiting effort.

Remember that Internet recruiting is only one segment of a high-performance recruiting plan.

Recruiting Agencies

Recruitment agencies help organizations attract qualified candidates. These companies offer expertise and creativity in finding talented personnel that may be available within your own organization. Because they concentrate on this area alone, they are more attuned to what strategies work. Generally, this service is not expensive since the agencies receive their commission from the media where they place ads.

Before proceeding with one of these organizations, however, it is best to investigate what each one can do for you. You might ask the following:

➤ How large is the agency? Does it have multiple offices? If your organization has several sites, can any of these be used?

➤ What do other clients say about this agency? Ask for and check references.

➤ How much lead-time does the agency need to prepare your campaign?

➤ What services are offered and which will be charged for? Some agencies offer extensive administrative services such as tracking advertising and results of campaigns. Will the company be charged for these extras? How much?

➤ How aggressive is the agency? In a tight labor market, more creative techniques must be used to attract candidates. Can this agency demonstrate a track record of innovative and unusual advertising that works?

➤ Does the agency demand a contract? If so, negotiate a trial period.

Recruiting Services

Recruiting services can be separated into four categories: employment agencies, temporary agencies, executive recruiters, and executive search firms or "head-hunters." The results of working these services can range from fruitful to disastrous depending on the relationship you develop. These organizations are in business to make money. Therefore, the faster they can fill a vacancy on commission, the more they profit. Unfortunately, the emphasis on speed can impair the quality of service. It is your responsibility as a client to define the parameters of the relationship and enforce quality control.

If the candidates being referred do not fit the position, turn them away. Agencies may try to give the "hard sell" for a candidate they think is a match. Mistakes due to impatience, panic, or even undue pressure can be costly at a later time.

Employment Agencies

These agencies may staff general personnel, but they often focus on a specific type of work group, such as clerical or technical staff. Employment agencies can exact their fee from the employee, the client company, or both. A good agency can save you time and money by screening applicants and providing only those who are qualified. Check the references of these organizations before you do business. Those that have been in business the longest are usually the best. Review your budget before committing to these services. Weigh the differences between paying an employment agency and using internal resources to recruit employees. Include in this analysis the cost of not filling the position quickly.

Temporary Agencies

These organizations are different from employment agencies in that they, rather than the client, pay the employee. Some enforce a monetary penalty on workers who accept a full-time position with a client. Large numbers of people work through "temp" agencies in today's work environment, so this may be a viable solution to your recruiting needs. These agencies can be found in the phone directory, but it is best to get referrals.

Executive Recruiters

These firms help companies find entry-level and mid-level managers. Their clients are primarily current job seekers. Executive recruiters base their income on successful matches between company and applicant. They work on either a retainer or contingency basis. Many specialize in a particular industry and can be most helpful, provided they have the necessary expertise. Working with an effective executive recruiter can save valuable time locating and screening likely applicants.

The cost of this service averages 30% of the new employee's first-year salary. This can be an expensive option, so look closely before committing. Executive recruiters can be located through phone directories, the classified ads section of the local paper, business directories, and referrals.

Professional/Executive Search Firms

Often called "headhunters," these companies hunt for corporate professionals or executives to fill senior positions in a client company. The process for conducting this type of search is complex. The headhunter begins by interviewing the company's management team and fully investigating its organization. These professionals usually specialize in one industry. Targeted professionals sought by headhunters are usually working managers in the field who can be lured away to a more challenging and lucrative position.

Compensation for these services averages 30% of first-year compensation. For most companies, the use of a headhunter is confined strictly to filling senior-level positions. Interview these agencies carefully before securing their services. This should be done in your office. Ask for references from current and previous clients.

College Placement Centers

College placement centers connect employers with qualified candidates to fill many needs. Interns and graduating students are an excellent source of state-of-the-art information and enthusiasm. Traditionally, only the larger companies have taken advantage of what these centers offer. But placement centers can be an excellent resource for smaller businesses as well. Just as you would conduct an advertising campaign to attract applicants to production jobs, you must publicize your existence to students. Visit with faculty and administrators to incorporate their help in spreading the word. Many students rely on these professionals for guidance in deciding where to work. Working with college placement centers is an especially helpful strategy in fields like engineering where demand for graduating students is high.

A college can also provide part-time help at less expense than the average employment agency. While college students must be paid, they are willing to work for less compensation in order to gain the practical experience and contacts. Call the placement office at your nearby college for additional information.

Public Job Services

It is likely that there are a variety of public job services in your community that maintain lists of candidates. These organizations are sometimes unjustly maligned. Some are state and federally supported, while professional associations and civic groups sponsor others. The most effective strategy for zeroing in on the best applicants is to develop a relationship with the counselors or coordinators of these organizations. They will help you select individuals to address your needs.

P A R T 4

Implementing Your Recruiting Plan

46

Placing Advertisements

Newspaper advertising is the most common means for announcing a vacancy. Unfortunately, it does not yield the desired results in many cases. What is put into a small space like this has to compete with hundreds of other openings. The ad must be attractive and specific. Even then, there is a good chance of receiving a number of unwanted résumés.

Before advertising in the local papers, peruse the classifieds. Observe their layout and where the type of job you want to fill is placed. If your type of opening cannot be found easily, you should look for another medium. Many cities have two papers. Many times the so-called blue-collar jobs are listed in one paper while white-collar jobs are listed in another. Placement tends to correlate with reader preference.

Besides the classifieds, you also have the option of placing a display ad. Much more can be done with a quarter, half, or full page of a newspaper. The special effects unavailable in the classified ad can be used here to attract greater attention.

But advertising studies have shown that small space ads will draw 75 to 80% of the response of a full page for much less cost. While classifieds do not stand out as much as a display ad, it is wise to refrain from inserting more than a quarter-page ad at any one time.

Avoid running a four-line ad in a major newspaper that is swallowed up by the ads surrounding it. Instead, place a display ad in a few local papers where your information will get more play. The extra space also allows the opportunity to add work-life issues to the job description and qualifications.

Consider advertising in other areas of the paper besides the employment section. Some companies have had success attracting older individuals, for instance, by placing ads on the obituary page.

In addition to local papers, there are regional and national publications that cater to a specific industry or profession. Unfortunately, these tend to be issued monthly or quarterly, and are not timely enough for the average opening. The one exception would be the large-scale campaign to recruit a sizable number of employees. But this takes substantial advance planning. Following is a checklist you can use to write an effective job notice and a sample job advertisement.

Vacancy Notice Checklist

Checkpoints to follow when writing a job notice:

- ❏ Begin the ad with a descriptive title. Make sure the title accurately reflects the job and is understandable to the reader.

- ❏ List necessary education and experience.

- ❏ Include a brief job description highlighting the most attractive points. Give the reader a perspective on how the job fits into the organization.

- ❏ Ask for a salary history. This information helps you screen out those who are under or over qualified.

- ❏ Sell the job benefits.

- ❏ Avoid colorful, but useless, adjectives. "Fast-paced" describes the environment. "Exciting" does not.

- ❏ Talk to the reader instead of simply listing duties. Help readers understand how much you care about hiring the right person.

- ❏ Eliminate unnecessary words and phrases. Get to the point. Quick-reading advertisements get read. Avoid abbreviations.

- ❏ Place yourself in the reader's position. What questions would you have about this job? Try to answer those concerns in the ad.

- ❏ You may want to omit your company's identity to avoid a deluge of un wanted applications or the responsibility of answering every response.

- ❏ How you want candidates to respond is up to you. For example, you may choose to ask telemarketing or customer service applicants to call so you can get a feel for their ability to communicate over the phone.

WRITING EFFECTIVE JOB ADVERTISEMENTS

Below are examples of poorly written job advertisements that were rewritten to be more attractive and specific. Practice writing effective job advertisements by rewriting the two examples in the second column in the spaces provided.

Poor

> Restaurant personnel needed for new Mexican restaurant. No experience necessary. Training provided. Apply between 2-4 at Burrito Bob's, 2222 S. Hampden Ave.

Poor

> Receptionist for dental office. Duties include phones and filing. Flexible hours. Send resume to Valley Dental, 3355 Market Street, San Francisco 94111.

Better

> **We Need You!**
>
> Restaurant Personnel
>
> Opening a new Mexican Restaurant in Southeast Denver. We're looking for high-energy individuals who enjoy a challenge. Experience is not necessary. We offer a complete training program. Sign up early and get the best hours!
>
> Apply in person between
> 2-4 p.m. weekdays at **Burrito Bob's,**
> 2222 S. Hampden Ave.

Better

Poor

> Office manager wanted for distribution center. Experienced only. Apply to:
> You Name It Gifts and Novelties
> 14 Girard Place, Suite 13-214
> Coral Gables, Florida 33407
> 646-4843

Poor

> Child-care assistant needed at busy center. Must have necessary qualifications and experience. Apply to: Little Sprouts Day Care, 1803 Prospect Street, Brooklyn.

Better

> **Office Manager**
> Manufacturer of novelties and gifts seeks a well-organized office manager for its distribution center. Two years experience managing others an absolute must. Word processing and electronic spreadsheet skills preferred. Distribution center experience a plus.
>
> Apply to:
> **You Name It Gifts and Novelties**
> 14 Girard Place, Suite 13-214
> Coral Gables, Florida 33407
> 646-4843

Better

Suggested Answers

Are you outgoing and detail-oriented?

Friendly dental office seeks receptionist for front office. Must have experience handling switchboard and juggling multiple tasks. Hours are flexible and office is centrally located. Dental benefits are top-notch!

Send resume and cover letter
with salary history to:
Valley Dental
3355 Market Street, San Francisco

Wanna Play?!

Join the team at Little Sprouts Day Care. Must be licensed and have 2-3 years experience with excellent references. Spanish-speaking a plus.

Apply in-person:
Little Sprouts Day Care
1803 Prospect Street, Brooklyn

Monitoring Costs

Hiring employees can be an expensive proposition, especially if costs are not monitored carefully.

But not all recruitment advertising has to cost money. Try innovative strategies for attracting applicants to your openings. Word-of-mouth is one of the most powerful tools available. Other mediums are discussed later in this chapter.

When budgeting for recruiting, do not forget to include indirect costs such as phone calls, administrative time, and interview time for line managers. In addition to these expenses, the new employee will need orientation and training to perform the job.

Occasionally calculate your company's recruiting and turnover costs. Combined, these two can be staggering. A little extra emphasis on retention and employee motivation can go a long way toward reducing recruiting expenses.

There are several areas that need to be taken into consideration, including overhead, staff time, phone expenses, and managerial time. Your costs may vary, depending on your location. Occasionally calculate your company's hiring costs to remind everyone of the substantial expense resulting from careless selection and improper training.

Saving Money

How can you save money in the recruiting process? Be practical and creative. Ask plenty of questions and approach the process with a commonsense perspective.

Costs can be reduced significantly if more attention is paid to the overall investment of time and expenditures. In many organizations, the recruiting process is not mobilized until a position needs to be filled. For instance, if an opening for a supervisor is filled in January and an opening for a similar type of position opens up three months later, a new recruiting campaign will most likely be initiated. A one-hour investment in calling those candidates involved in the process last time may reveal two or three prescreened individuals who are still interested.

A policy of "we are always looking for good people" even though there may be no openings at the time can save backbreaking work when someone is needed in a hurry. Encouraging employees to be on the lookout for possible applicants not only builds candidate pools, but investment in the organization. Besides, it does not cost a thing!

It is best to start from the beginning when developing recruiting procedures. Examine every step and ask, "How can I save money and still accomplish this task effectively?" Here are a few hints to help you:

➤ **Look to internal referrals first, whenever possible.** This could save a good portion of out-of-pocket recruiting costs.

➤ **Concentrate on local hiring.** There is no reason to pursue out-of-state candidates if someone suitable can be found in your own back yard.

➤ **Be extremely judicious in the use of headhunters and employment agencies.** You are not necessarily saving money or getting the better candidate. Check references and reputation before proceeding.

➤ **Keep a constant eye on costs.** Remind those doing the hiring that recruiting is a cost center. Cut corners when you can. Following is a sample memo detailing the costs of recruiting for a management position. This will give you an idea of how to break down costs associated with a new hire.

Memorandum

To: Jack Clark, Vice President Production
From: Ralph Needick, Operations

Here is the final breakdown on replacing Sue Green, our manager of distribution.

Cash Expenses
Classified advertising (three display ads for one week) $ 975
Postage, phone, copying, miscellaneous   75

Labor @ V.P.'s and managers' time (average $37/hour)
Search planning meetings (5 hours)   185
Development & placement of ads (2 hours)   74
Review of applications (2 hours)   74
Phone interviews (16 hours)   592
Second interviews (8 hours)   296
Decision making (3 hours)   111
Negotiation (5 hours)   185
Orientation and planning (10 hours)   370
Training (40 hours over 3 months)   1480
Miscellaneous administration (5 hours)   185

Staff time (average $12/hour)
Search administration (30 hours)   360
Secretarial support (20 hours)   240
Orientation and training support (10 hours)   120

GRAND TOTAL $5322

Recruiting Media

There are many ways to reach applicants, from the traditional to the outrageous. Here is a collection of ideas that have worked to attract substantial numbers of applicants. Keep in mind that different labor groups respond to different messages. Your job is to find the matches.

Airplane banners attract attention at large events or gatherings.

Billboards can be placed in strategic locations, such as close to a competitor's site.

Bumper stickers get exposure whenever the car is on the road.

Career fairs are a great place to display your company to a wide or narrow audience, depending on the fair's target.

Cinema billboards get the attention of young workers and seniors.

Direct mail can garner the attention of a large number of potential applicants in a specific locale or profession.

Door hangers are effective where the recruiting is geographically limited, such as a college campus or retirement complex.

Envelope stuffers can be used to reach your customers who may generate referrals since they already use your products.

Job fairs are a good way to showcase your organization.

Kiosks offer an opportunity to advertise in high traffic areas. You can also purchase portable kiosks to increase your exposure.

Leaflets that are aggressively written with easy contact instructions will capture the attention of those leading busy lives.

Magnetic business cards or die-cut graphics could be enclosed with recruiting literature. Potential employees may post them in a visible place, creating a constant reminder about your organization.

Open houses give the public an opportunity to see how your organization works. Set up a table at the end of the tour to encourage applications.

Point-of-sale materials, distributed in retail stores, are convenient ways to catch customers who might be interested in working for your company.

Posters with tear-off coupons make it easy for potential applicants to fill out a short form and send it in.

Presentations to local groups by any employee should include a pitch about working for the company.

Radio can be tailored to the audience. Besides commercials, companies can use public service announcements and appearances on talk shows.

Restaurant place mats announce to a captive audience that the establishment is hiring.

Table tents also can grab the attention of restaurant patrons.

Telemarketing can be extremely effective if the pitch is prepared and executed correctly. This is generally used to access targeted audiences.

Television, especially during late night and daytime hours, can be very effective at reaching out-of-work applicants.

Trade shows, while not geared toward recruiting, provide an excellent opportunity to reach individuals in a particular field.

Transit advertising accesses commuters working in your vicinity. It demonstrates that they can reach your company without needing a car.

Developing Labor Pools for the Future

Organizations that will thrive in the future must be proactive in their development of consistent labor pools. This development must be implemented now and take place continually.

Here are a few key strategies for ensuring your workforce of the future:

➤ **Make sure recruiting awareness is a way of life for all employees.** This will ensure a constant stream of referrals. Reward those who do refer.

➤ **Maintain positive employee relations both inside and outside the organization.***

➤ **Continue to build corporate image at every opportunity.** Maintain a constant flow of information about programs and special events taking place in the company.

➤ **Anticipate changes in the community's demographics and therefore its labor force.** Do not follow what the media are saying. Find out before they do!

➤ **Closely monitor applications.** Look for patterns in response from certain labor groups. This will provide keys to where you should concentrate your advertising.

➤ **Maintain your aggressiveness in the pursuit of applicants.** Be creative and try the unusual to attract attention.

➤ **Hire the best when they appear.** Even if you do not have an exact spot, do what you can to get them on board and take advantage of their enthusiasm and skills.

➤ **Get rid of employees who do not produce.** These individuals have a negative impact on the teamwork and energy of those who do. Consequently, applicants and new hires will develop the wrong impression of organizational culture.

Know your organization's strategic plan and where you'll have openings in the next 12 months. Anticipation of need eliminates panic.

*For more information on maintaining positive employee relations, read *Retaining Your Employees* by Barb Wingfield and Janice Berry, Crisp Publications.

S U M M A R Y

58

Strategies for Attracting Applicants

Here are some strategies that have been used successfully by a variety of organizations for attracting applicants. While some may appear too bold or unusual at first glance, take a minute to consider how each one might be applied to your recruiting effort.

Ads featuring top workers. Ads with pictures featuring productive employees send the message that your organization cares about its workers. The employees featured will get a charge out of the attention.

Appreciation programs. Hold an annual event recognizing employees. Give awards. Have fun. And make sure it is covered in the local press.

Cash awards. Cold cash is a great motivator. Publicly reward employees who bring in referrals.

Celebrity-hosted events. Ask or hire a local celebrity to host a plant tour, new product rollout, or other event. Once the crowd is attracted, go to work recruiting employees.

Collateral in foreign languages. Print your recruiting posters and materials in languages of the local community. This demonstrates goodwill and enhances the number of possible applicants.

Commuter rail and bus passes. For those in low-income areas, free commuting can be a significant incentive. Tokens and passes usually can be purchased at quantity discounts.

Competing personnel. Keep an eye on top performers in competing organizations. While you don't want to encourage the pirating of employees, their restlessness may be to your advantage if they're looking for a change.

Customer advertisements. Customers who know and use your products can become reliable employees. Make sure they are aware of openings. Posting signs in a store and stuffing bills with position announcements are effective strategies.

Customer referrals. Ask customers to refer applicants. You might even offer incentives such as discount coupons.

Dead résumé file. Don't throw out those old résumés. Phoning applicants from six months ago may garner new interest.

Diversity training. Train all managers to adapt to the new diversity in the work force. This skill is essential for supervisors and recruiters.

Drawings for cash prizes. Consider a program where successful new hires are made eligible for a cash drawing provided they stay a specified period of time.

Full benefits for part-timers. This can be very attractive to single parents. While this can be expensive, you can achieve better retention along with loyal workers.

High school and college shepherd program. Develop a program to assist minorities by providing tutoring and financial assistance. In addition, you can provide summer jobs and eventually entice them into working full-time for your firm. This is a long-term investment with a long-term reward.

Hot air balloons. These generally attract a great amount of attention. Tether one in a parking lot or field outside your plant.

Interns. High school and college interns are an excellent source of immediate human resources and an opportunity to see potential employees in action.

Job-opportunity brochures. Develop a brochure describing the employment opportunities within your company and make sure that all employees have a few to distribute.

Job shares. Allow two individuals to share the same position. This can be very attractive to skilled applicants with commitments at home.

Keep in touch with those who leave. Follow up on good employees who leave for other positions. Send them a periodic post card or note. Former employees may want to return in the future, and they already know your system.

Layered advertising. Some companies use advertisements that draw applicants in by making a bold statement at the top and then lead into information about the job. One organization, for instance, ran an ad with the words "temporary sanity" at the top to attract those looking for part-time work.

Media promotions. Team up with local radio or television stations to promote the company using gimmicks, contests, or drawings. Have staff ready to answer questions and recruit applicants.

Mini-applications. While more gimmick than application, miniature "business-card-size" applications grab the attention of potential applicants. Ask all employees to carry them.

Mobile recruiting vans. Rent a van and set up a mobile recruiting station at the local mall or movie theater. Find ways to go to the applicants instead of asking them to come to you.

On-site interviews. Rent a storefront or kiosk in the local mall and solicit applications from passersby.

"Open-air" sessions. Conduct periodic meetings with current employees for the purposes of hashing out concerns and grievances. While these meetings may be quiet at first, employees will open up after a while and speak out. This is also an excellent time to ask staff for ideas on recruiting applicants. Make sure these meetings are reported in the press. A company with an open atmosphere breeds interest.

Outplacement pools. Stay aware of organizations that might be downsizing. Ask if you can speak to employees who are being laid off.

Parking lots. Advertise that you have close-in parking lots for night shifts. This will relieve the apprehension by some that it might be dangerous to work at your company at night.

Part-time workers. Examine whether you need to fill all new openings with full-time workers. Can one or two part-time employees do the same job? Part-timers save you money and are easier to find.

Personalized advertisements. Rather than placing a traditional classified advertisement, try a more personalized approach: "We'll miss you, Susan! Susan has been our accounts receivable clerk for the past five years and now she's leaving. She is skilled at handling receivables of up to $300,000 per month, can budget for her department, and is able to fill in as bookkeeper when needed. If you think you would like to take Susan's place in this fast-paced, but fun atmosphere, call Bob at 574-7468 before Friday!"

Recruiting slogans. Develop a slogan that grabs the attention of the group you are recruiting. The Los Angeles Police Department used the slogan, "Be Somebody! Be a Cop!"

Referrals from applicants. Ask applicants for the names and phone numbers of other individuals they know who might be interested in a job. They might like to work with their friends.

Referrals on applications. Include a space on applications for applicants to list others who might be interested in working for your organization.

Rehire former employees. Be willing to re-hire former employees if they apply. While a few may be undesirable, most will fit right in and already know your systems, which saves training.

Relocation. Consider providing a stipend to a superior candidate to assist with moving expenses. This is a common practice for hiring executives.

Retiree job bank. Develop a list of retirees who might be interested in working at their old job from time to time. Companies that have tried this say it works extremely well.

Return postage. Always provide return postage for applications. You don't want to lose good candidates because they don't have the money for a stamp.

School relations. Develop better relations with the schools in your area. They can be a tremendous source of labor and referrals. Offer to make presentations. Contribute equipment and sponsor events and contests. Through these activities, you can develop a positive reputation.

Shared housing. In locales where housing is in short supply, offer shared housing to accommodate new employees and those working temporarily.

Sign-on bonuses. This has been common practice for executives, but the offer of an extra $50 may sway good lower-level candidates from taking other positions.

Site tours. If your organization is a source of fascination in the community, use this to your advantage. Offer tours on a periodic basis and place a table with applications at the end.

Slang in ads and posters. Build the current slang into recruitment advertising when attracting adolescents. The more they identify with your organization, the more they will apply and tell others.

Sponsored entertainment. Sponsor entertainment, parties, and the like to attract applicants. As with any gimmick, it is up to you to recruit interested individuals once they've arrived.

Subsidized housing. In wealthy areas, subsidized housing eases applicant apprehensions about finding a place to live.

Teacher unions and school districts. Consult with these organizations to locate teachers who are interested in part- or full-time summer employment.

Telecommuting. A number of companies have begun to allow employees to work at home some or all of the time. These companies provide the necessary materials and equipment and the employee benefits from not having to commute and being available to attend to family needs.

Telephone job line. Install a phone line dedicated to announcing current openings. Potential applicants can call the line periodically to check for new openings.

Temporary workers. Consider the use of temporary staff in more than clerical positions. A temporary operations manager can set up a new production line without your organization having to hire another full-time person.

Tenure awards. Give awards to employees who pass certain marks in attendance. McDonald's restaurants recognize their employees with an attendance pin after the first three months at work.

Toll-free number. Encourage candidates from long distances to phone toll-free. The modest cost of this service is overcome by the goodwill extended to potential applicants.

Training sessions. Some companies offer training courses to potential applicants. The applicants gain by receiving training on particular equipment and the company gets trained employees if they pass the course.

Two-timing employees. Ask current employees to take on a second job such as custodian or maintenance engineer. You will have a reliable employee and this person earns the extra money desired.

Un-retire employees. Approach the retirees of other firms who performed tasks they could perform in your company. Many will be anxious to get back to work, at least part-time.

Van services. Provide van service to employees having to commute through less desirable areas or at night. This provides goodwill and reduces insurance risk.

Visiting executives. Ask your executives to make presentations in the community on the organization's need for qualified people. This information should be included in any presentations they make to any group. This works especially well if they have achieved some notoriety or fame.

Additional Reading

Andler, Edward C. *The Complete Reference Checking Handbook.* NY: AMACOM, 1998.

Fitzwater, Terry. *Behavior-Based Interviewing.* Boston, MA: Thomson Learning/ NETg, 2000.

Hayes, David and Jack Ninemeier. *50 One-Minute Tips for Recruiting Employees.* Boston, MA: Thomson Learning/NETg, 2001.

Ling, Barbara. *Poor Richard's Internet Recruiting.* Lakewood, CO: Top Floor Publishing, 2001.

Steingold, Fred S. *The Employer's Legal Handbook,* Fourth Edition. Berkeley, CA: Nolo Press, 2000.

Wendover, Robert. *High Performance Hiring.* Boston, MA: Thomson Learning/ NETg, 2003.

Wendover, Robert. *Smart Hiring: The Complete Guide to Recruiting Employees.* Naperville, IL: Sourcebooks, Inc., 2002.

Wingfield, Barb and Janice Berry. *Retaining Your Employees.* Boston, MA: Thomson Learning/NETg, 2001.

Other Resources

Periodicals

HR Magazine
Society for Human Resource Management
606 N. Washington St.
Alexandria, VA 22314
(703) 548-3440

Workforce Magazine
245 Fischer Ave., Suite B2
Costa Mesa, CA 92626
(714) 751-1883

Inc. Magazine
38 Commercial Wharf
Boston, MA 02110
(617) 248-8000

Employment Practice Reference Sources

Bureau of National Affairs
9435 Key West Ave.
Rockville, MD 20850
1-800-372-1033

Business and Legal Reports
141 Mill Rock Road E.
Old Saybrook, CT 06475
(203) 245-7448

CCH Inc.
4025 W. Perterson Ave.
Chicago, IL 60646-6085
1-800-835-5224

Dartnell Inc.
360 Hiatt Drive
Palm Beach Gardens, FL 33418
1-800-621-5463
(561) 662-6520

Equal Employment Opportunity Commission
1801 L Street N.W.
Washington, DC 20507
(202) 663-4900

Personnel Forms

Amsterdam Printing & Litho
Wallins Corner Road
Amsterdam, NY 12010
(518) 842-6000

Dartnell Inc.
360 Hiett Road
Palm Beach Gardens, FL 33418
1-800-621-5463
(516) 662-6520

Selectform Inc.
P. O. Box 3045
Freeport, NY 11520
(516) 623-0400